Cars

McLaren 720S

JULIA GARSTECKI

🌐 WORLD BOOK

This World Book edition of *McLaren 720S*
is published by agreement between
Black Rabbit Books and World Book, Inc.
© 2020 Black Rabbit Books,
2140 Howard Dr. West,
North Mankato, MN 56003 U.S.A.
World Book, Inc.,
180 North LaSalle St., Suite 900,
Chicago, IL 60601 U.S.A.

Marysa Storm, editor; Catherine Cates, interior designer;
Grant Gould, cover designer; Omay Ayres, photo researcher

Library of Congress Control Number: 2018017373

ISBN: 978-0-7166-3945-9

Printed in the United States. 1/19

Image Credits
media.mclarenautomotive.
com: McLaren Media, Cover (car),
1, 4–5, 6, 8–9, 10–11, 12, 14 (btm),
14–15, 15 (btm), 17, 18, 20–21, 23, 24,
24–25, 26, 28–29; Shutterstock: Andrew
Harker, 15 (top); Christopher Lyzcen, 32; Ele-
namiv, Cover (bkgd); i viewfinder,
14 (top); Philip Pilosian, 3; Sucharn
Wetthayasapha, 26–27; tokkoro.com:
McLaren Automotive, 31
Every effort has been made to contact
copyright holders for material reproduced
in this book. Any omissions will
be rectified in subsequent
printings if notice is given
to the publisher.

Contents

CHAPTER 1

Racing Down
the Road. 4

CHAPTER 2

Design. 10

CHAPTER 3

Power and
Performance. 22

CHAPTER 4

An Epic Car. 29

Other Resources. 30

Racing
Down the Road

The McLaren 720S rolls onto the track. Finally, the driver can unleash the car's true power. With a press of the gas pedal, the supercar speeds off. Roaring, it races through the course, showing off its beauty and strength.

COMPARING METRIC HORSEPOWER

2018 Ferrari 812 Superfast

800

Like a Shark

McLaren revealed the 720S in 2017. The supercar's name comes from its 720 metric **horsepower**. It is part of the British company's Super Series. The 720S thrills drivers. Like a great white shark, the car is **sleek** and strong. Few cars can match its power and look.

2018 Lamborghini Aventador S	2018 McLaren 720S	2018 Porsche 911 GT3
740	720	500

WHEELS

SLEEK SHAPE

SLIM HEADLIGHTS

LOW BODY

Y19 MCL

GB

CARS McLAREN PRESS

9

CHAPTER 2

Design

The 720S has an **aerodynamic** design. To perfect the design, the 720S went through hundreds of hours of testing. **Engineers** used a wind tunnel to see how air hit the car. The 720S' shape directs wind to create **downforce**. Downforce increases a car's grip. It makes the car more stable.

McLaren used features from sharks and race cars in the 720S' design.

The doors channel air to the radiators.
Radiators help cool the engine.

Designer Doors

The 720S' doors are different than regular doors. They don't swing out. Instead, they open forward and up. The doors include part of the roof. Their design makes it easier to enter and exit the car. They let drivers park the cars in tight spots too.

MANY CHOICES

Buyers have many options when getting a 720S.

34
EXTERIOR COLORS

3
RIM OPTIONS

8
BRAKE CALIPER COLORS

2
SEAT TYPES

Amazing Headlights

The 720S has Static Adaptive Headlights. They direct light based on steering. When the car enters a curve, the headlights adjust to light the road. They increase visibility.

The steering wheel is simple. It doesn't have buttons like most other steering wheels.

Simple and Strong

The 720S has a clean interior. The display looks like it does in most other supercars. But it can enter Slim Display Mode. In this mode, the screen tilts forward. It becomes smaller. The driver can still see important information, such as speed. But the screen isn't distracting.

The Monocage II

The 720S has many cool features. One of them is the Monocage II. It's one big piece of carbon fiber. This tub makes up much of the car's body.

Carbon fiber is expensive. For a unique look, buyers can order extra carbon fiber features.

Carbon fiber is tough and light. Less is needed to make a car strong. Thanks to its strength, pillars between the windows are narrow. Narrow pillars means better visibility.

CHAPTER 3

Power and Performance

The 720S has a top speed of 212 miles (341 kilometers) per hour. An amazing 4-liter V-8 engine helps the car reach this speed. Its two **turbochargers** give it a powerful boost.

· ·

The engine bay glows with a red light.

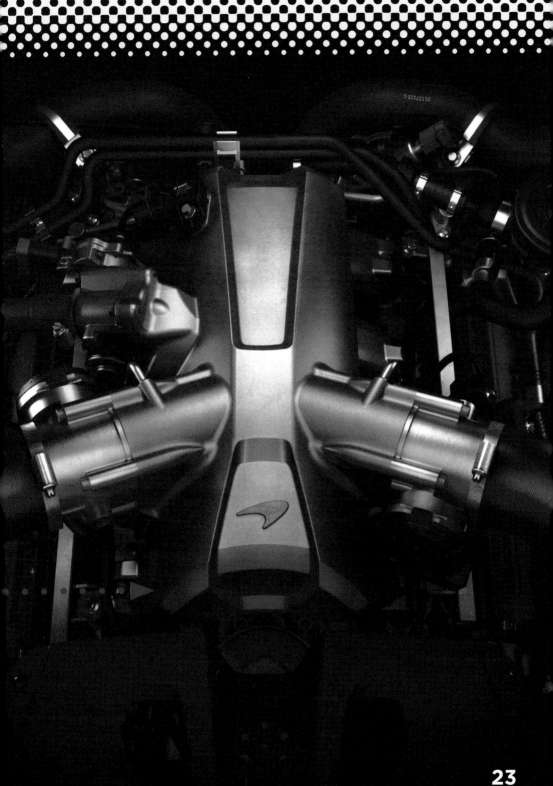

Fantastic Features

Many drivers like to customize their drive. The 720S lets them do just that. Drivers can change the cars' traction. They choose how strongly the cars grip the road. With less traction, drivers can **drift**.

2

TOTAL SEATING

By the Numbers

$288,845

BASE PRICE

178.9
INCHES
(454.4 CENTIMETERS)
LENGTH

47.1
INCHES
(119.6 CM)
HEIGHT

TIME TO GO FROM
0 to 60 MILES
(97 KM) PER HOUR

2.8
SECONDS

The 720S has won many awards. In 2017, it won Most Beautiful Supercar of the Year.

CHAPTER 4

An Epic Car

The 720S is smooth and fast. Turn it on, and the car sounds as powerful as it looks. Every one of the body's lines has a purpose. Its engine is a piece of art. This car will impress drivers for years to come.

19 MCL

CARS.MCLAREN.PRESS

aerodynamic (air-oh-dahy-NAM-ik)—something that is shaped so it moves easily through air

caliper (KAL-uh-per)—a device used to press a brake pad against the sides of a brake rotor

downforce (doun-FAWRS)—a force that increases the stability and grip of a motor vehicle by pressing it downward

drift (DRIFT)—to break traction with the back of the car and slide through a curve

engineer (ehn-juh-NEER)—a designer or builder

horsepower (HORS-pow-uhr)—a unit used to measure the power of engines

sleek (SLEEK)—straight and smooth

turbocharger (TUR-bo-charj-uhr)—a device that increases an engine's power by using its exhaust to force air into the engine

BOOKS

Bailey, Devon. *Supercars: A Celebration of Iconic Marques*. Broomall, PA: Mason Crest, 2016.

Bodensteiner, Peter. *Supercars*. Gearhead Garage. Mankato, MN: Black Rabbit Books, 2017.

Fishman, Jon M. *Cool Sports Cars*. Awesome Rides. Minneapolis: Lerner Publications, 2019.

WEBSITES

McLaren 720S Reviews
www.caranddriver.com/mclaren/720s

McLaren 720S Super Series
720s.mclaren.com/us

McLaren 720S - Super Series
cars.mclaren.com/super-series/720s

INDEX

A

acceleration, 27

awards, 28

B

brakes, 15

C

carbon fiber, 20–21

cooling, 12

costs, 26

D

designs, 7, 8–9, 10, 11,
    12, 13, 14–15, 16,
    18, 19, 20–21, 22,
    26–27, 29

E

engines, 12, 22, 29

H

headlights, 16

horsepower, 6–7

S

speeds, 22

steering, 16